KETTERING REVISITED

Grant of Arms by the Earl Marshal and Hereditary Marshal of
England, dated 26 September 1938.

William Farey's photograph of Gold Street in 1868, including the newly-completed Fuller Church

KETTERING REVISITED
Pictures from the Past

Tony Smith

W.D. WHARTON
Wellingborough

The author dedicates this book
to the people of Kettering
and, in particular, to his late parents
Joan and Rodger Smith

First published in 1993 by
W.D. Wharton
37 Sheep Street
Wellingborough
Northamptonshire NN8 1BX

ISBN 0 9518557 3 5

Designed and typeset by John Hardaker, Wollaston, Northamptonshire
Printed and bound in Great Britain by
Woolnough Bookbinding Ltd
Irthlingborough, Northamptonshire

Contents

Foreword by Tony Ireson 7

Kettering ~ the Town and its People 8

Victorian Kettering 10

Edwardian and Georgian Kettering 17

High Street 33

Gold Street 48

Market Place 62

Newland Street/Silver Street 74

Dalkeith Place and Horsemarket 85

London Road 93

Rockingham Road 102

Wicksteed Park 108

More Street Scenes 120

People and Events 139

Kettering District 167

Acknowledgements

All illustrations in this book come from the author's private archives. Main text sources include: F.W. Bull's *History of Kettering*; *Kettering British Industries, 1891*; *Kettering Temp George V, 1912*; *Kelly's Directory of Northamptonshire* (various); *Lost and Hidden Kettering* and *A Walk Around Kettering*, Kettering Civic Society; *Souvenir of the Kettering Charter of Incorporation, 1938*; and *A Pictorial History of Kettering*, The Rotary Club of Kettering Huxloe, 1985.

Sincere thanks to Mr Tony Ireson for writing the foreword and providing much of the inspiration for this project.

Front end-paper captions
(Left) An Edwardian view of Kettering railway station.
(Right) Gold Street during the 1920s.

Back end-paper captions
(Left) Bird's-eye view of Church Walk, showing Kettering Rectory and the old Police Station ~ 1925.
(Right) The old Grammar School building during the 1950s.

Kettering Parish Church circa 1900.

Foreword
'Our beloved Old Kettering'

I don't mind admitting that I sat up into the small hours looking at these historic pictures. Besides depicting our beloved Old Kettering, they are fascinating for technical reasons. First, a computer scanning process has enhanced them, as well as enlarging them to full-page size. Second, this is a newspaperman's book. Tony has edited the pictures, picking out the human interest and presenting it irresistibly.

As well as bringing back our own youth, the collection shows hauntingly the life-scenes and values of our parents and grandparents, and I don't just mean buildings. We see, for example, bikes left at kerbs with no fear of theft, shops beautified by elegant fascia boards, a girl leaning on her cycle listening to a street organ where today a pedestrian risks being killed in the traffic rush, and ~ the reverse of the medal ~ a disabled man making the best of things, faithfully attended by his dog.

Tony has wisely limited his captions to a few words of identification. We shall all supply our own captions: the heartbreak witnessed by the old Workhouse; our youthful days of joy thanks to Charles Wicksteed; adventurous all-weather trips on open-top buses; reunions in the homely little pubs that dotted the town; and the Central Hall, and all that went with it. I need not continue ~ you will.

We will all have a favourite picture. Mine is the mystery World War I scene on the Market Place [page 146]. My guess is the crowd and soldiers are waiting for the clergy to arrive to begin the Day of Prayer called by George V in 1918 when things were desperate on the Western Front. Like all the pictures, it will provoke much discussion.

I commend this book, warmly congratulate its author, for whom it crowns many years of work, and am sure *Kettering Revisited* will be bought, read and always treasured.

Tony Ireson
Kettering
1993

7

Kettering ~ the Town and its People

Many people reading this will have been born and raised in Kettering, like the author, and will still live in the town; some will have moved away but remain in touch with friends and relatives; others may have been brought into the area through marriage or employment and come to love Kettering as their home town.

Some may know Kettering through visiting friends here, or have enjoyed themselves at Wicksteed Park; they may even have watched a football match here. Everyone will have their own impressions and, it is hoped, happy memories of a Midlands town of great spirit, a town steeped in history.

As a borough, Kettering dates from 29 September 1938, but it was first mentioned in the year 956 when its name appeared as Cytringan in a charter of King Edwy granting the Manor Aelfsige.

In AD 972 King Edgar granted "Kyteringas" to certain Monks of Medeshamstede. Their ownership was confirmed in the Domesday Book in 1086 where the name appears as Cateringe. In the seventeenth century the town came into the hands of the Rockingham and Montagu families, who still have connections with it.

In the year 1227 Henry III granted a charter allowing the manor to hold a market "every seventh day on Friday". The charter also gave permission to hold one fair every year to last eight days ~ later known as Kettering Feast, a tradition still honoured every June.

Built of Barnack stone, Kettering's parish church of SS Peter and Paul is one of the most impressive in the county. Its lofty spire, rising from its tower to a height of 178 feet, has watched over the town for more than 500 years and, dominating the town's skyline, is a landmark for miles around.

William Carey (1761-1834)

The borough has yet wider associations with religious life, since in 1792 it became the birthplace of the Baptist Missionary Society. Respected local minister Andrew Fuller, and the group's first missionary William Carey were among the select few at that historic first meeting at a house in Lower Street.

Another famous missionary was William Knibb. Born in Market Street in 1803, he served in Jamaica where he became a pioneer of the abolition of slavery in the colonies. The borough coat of arms depicts his cause by showing a negro slave with a broken chain hanging from his wrist (see page 1).

Baptist minister John Gill, born here in 1697, was a writer of no mean merit, having been the author of famous expositions on the Song of Solomon and the Old and New Testaments.

In the world of art Kettering produced three out-

The Revd Andrew Fuller (1754-1815)

Abolitionist William Knibb
(1803-1845)

Charles Wicksteed
(1847-1931)

standing men ~ John Trivett Nettleship (1841), Thomas Cooper Gotch (1854) and Sir Alfred East (1849), the latter giving his name to the town's art gallery in Sheep Street.

But possibly the town's best-loved benefactor was Charles Wicksteed, the engineer who bought land to create a free pleasure park for children which opened to the public in 1921. Today Wicksteed Park is enjoyed by thousands of families who flock by the coachload from all over the country.

During the last century the name of Kettering became known far and wide, providing people with clothes for their backs and shoes for their feet. In more recent years the exploits of the town's football team, the Poppies, put the town firmly on the sporting map.

The advent of the railway in May 1857 did much to bring prosperity to the district, later providing vital links with London and major Midlands cities.

There are now hopes that current road projects, in particular the opening of the A1-M1 link, will herald a new era of development and commerce in an expanding area.

Almost daily, it seems, the face of Kettering is altering as the town and its residents adapt to the increasing needs and demands of our modern world.

In the space of my lifetime many fine old buildings have sadly disappeared in the name of progress, including Beech House, the old Grammar School and the Post Office buildings in Gold Street, to the regret of many who have treasured the town's heritage.

This book takes a loving, lingering look back at a vanished world, when the pace of life seemed less hurried, and the streets of Kettering echoed to the laughter of children and the clatter of horses' hooves. I sincerely hope readers enjoy this pictorial parade through history as much as I have enjoyed compiling it.

Tony Smith

One of Kettering's most famous families, the Gotches. Top left: artist Thomas Cooper Gotch; top right: shoemaker Henry Gale Gotch (after whom the school is named); bottom left: architect John Alfred Gotch; bottom right: School Board Chairman Davis Frederick Gotch; centre: Miss Jessica Gotch.

Victorian Kettering

Kettering High Street in 1898, looking back towards the Market Place. Joseph Emerson's café and confectionery shop, demolished for road widening in 1901, was replaced by the Northants Union Bank building (now NatWest). The business moved to Sheep Street, where it earned a first-class reputation for garden party catering.

Market Street in 1897. The shop in the centre was the birthplace of the famous missionary William Knibb in 1803, and belonged to his father, who was a draper. On the right is Mr Bagshaw's fish and poultry shop, which was later demolished and replaced by The Sun Hotel.

The old Duke's Arms in Market Street was one of the town's great inns, built
in 1667 and demolished in 1879. The site, once a yarn market in the
seventeenth century, was later occupied by Barnett & Soans, Electricians
and Burgess & Jeffries, Solicitors.

A photograph of Workhouse Lane in the 1890s. This was later renamed Dryland Street after the late Dr Winter Dryland, whose surgery was established next to the old Evening Telegraph offices.

Kettering Industrial Co-operative Society, founded in 1866, made a significant contribution to the life of the town. This picture shows the magnificent frontage of the Newland Street drapery shortly after it opened in 1893.

A fine view of the corner of Gold Street and Newland Street in the 1890s showing W.H. Baker's shop selling clothing and carpets. The thatched building was W. Bryant's fruit shop.

The old houses in Hazelwood Lane, named after Farmer Hazelwood, who
once lived there. The house with people outside was a meeting place for the
Independent Church in 1689 in the days of the Revd John Maydwell's
ministry. It was the home of his granddaughter in 1666 and
was demolished in 1955.

The two-storey premises of W.E. and J. Goss, the printers, stationers and
bookbinders, at the corner of High Street and Market Street. The printing
works were in the High Street, connected by private phone to the Market
Street premises. The frontage was demolished for road-widening in 1900.

Edwardian and Georgian Kettering

The lack of heavy road traffic enabled local people to stroll gently along
Dalkeith Place in 1915 without fear of being knocked over.

A resident of this old cottage in George Street clears snow in this wintry
picture looking up towards the Parish Church in April 1908.

A beat bobby (centre) mingles with the crowds on Kettering market in 1906.

The clip-clop of a pony and trap echoes along the High Street in this
atmospheric photograph from 1912.

Two views of the town library from the Headlands, both taken in 1910. The art gallery wasn't built for another three years.

Cyclists join buses and lorries in a bustling Sheep Street in 1924.

Two pictures of Carey Mission House in Lower Street, birthplace of the Baptist Missionary Society in 1792. William Carey, a former cobbler, set up the first mission in India.

Baptist Missionary Society
Bicentenary logo.

The historic ceremony from 1909 (above) when the Revd J.B. Myers, in top hat, unveiled the Mission House plaque which can still be seen today (right).
In 1992 parties of Americans visited Kettering to join in the 200th anniversary celebrations.

In This House on Octr 2ND 1792
A meeting was held to form a society for propagating the Gospel among the Heathen, and £13.2s.6d. was contributed for that purpose. Andrew Fuller was elected Secretary and Reynold Hogg Treasurer. William Carey, to whose sermon at Nottingham in May of the same year, the movement was due, embarked for India on June 13th 1793. This meeting marks the founding of the Baptist Missionary Society and the inauguration of Modern Foreign Missions.

The Toller Congregational Chapel, erected in Gold Street in 1723 and radically altered in 1849 and 1875. Its name commemorates the Revd Thomas Northcote Toller and his son Thomas, who between them ministered there for 100 years (1775-1875).

The Royal Hotel, 1906. Formerly the White Hart, its name was changed in 1844 to mark the brief stop there by Queen Victoria en route to Burghley House, Stamford. It was rebuilt in 1878 and sold in 1896 by the Duke of Buccleuch, who had bought it as the Conservative headquarters for the elections of the old North Northants constituency.

A cloaked figure passes the Northamptonshire Union Bank (now NatWest) in this High Street photograph from 1916.

Two views from opposite ends of Northampton Road in the days before private houses and the United Counties bus garage were built. The sheep picture was taken near the junction with Station Road in 1908.

More sheep being driven into town in 1906 on what later became the A43 to Northampton. This was taken from the bridge looking away from the town.

Kettering Library in 1914, and in front is the memorial to Dr John Winter Dryland, designed by John Alfred Gotch and erected in 1907. Sadly the troughs on either side were removed when horses were ousted by the motor car.

Kettering Free Library remains one of the town's finest buildings. It was built in 1904 for £8,450 thanks to the generosity of the well-known benefactor Andrew Carnegie. By 1910 it had 7,312 books for loan. The town's earlier library had been in the Corn Exchange on the Market Place in 1896.

The Alfred East Art Gallery, also designed by J.A. Gotch, was opened on 31 July 1913 by Earl Spencer. Between the gallery and the library is a bust of the artist (1849-1913), who died a few weeks after the opening of the building which bore his name and held the art collection he gave to the town.

A 'Bullnose' Morris car is parked outside the Art Gallery in Sheep Street during the late 1920s – long before double yellow lines were introduced!

The awning of Pritchards the drapers, next to the Royal Hotel, is seen on the
left of this High Street scene from 1915. Note the horse emerging
from Market Street on the right.

High Street

A super shot of High Street traffic in 1908. On the right we see a cripple
hobbling past the bank with his dog.

These two High Street views are taken from the same spot but show very different forms of transport ~ early motor cars replacing the humble horse and carriage by the 1920s.

A man pushes his barrow in the foreground of this High Street picture from
around 1910.

Two postmen (left) and a boy with a hoop (right) feature in this street-scene
from 1921.

A delivery boy with his empty load is the main feature in this peaceful scene
near Lloyds Bank on the corner of Market Street in 1907.

A typical early 1900s scene outside the Royal Hotel. Note the baskets of luggage on the pavement outside.

A group of local schoolgirls with their straw hats gather near the corner of
Market Street in 1924.

An old Austin 10 is parked in front of Barclays Bank in the late 1930s. At the corner of Market Street is Boots the chemist, built in 1894. The building was eventually demolished to make way for a new Barclays.

A Rover 16 is parked near the same spot in this photograph ~ also from the 1930s.

A fine reminder of the early days of motoring in this picture of High Street and Market Place. Outside the Royal Hotel, advertising its garage facilities, is a horse-drawn vehicle.

Two rather more modern views of the High Street, taken during the early 1950s. One shows the Regal Cinema (later Granada) and a sale at Hepworths the tailors opposite. The cinema opened on Boxing Day 1936, could seat 1,700 people and was famous for its stage shows. It finally became a bingo hall in the mid-1970s.

This 1910 picture, looking towards the former Bakehouse Hill, reveals that the sale at Webb Bros' Central Clothing Store was due to end on 17 September.

The impressive frontage of Webb Bros. Founded in 1789, it had branches in ten other towns at one point, and bought new premises in Market Street in 1927.

The Electric Pavilion, facing Gold Street, was officially opened on Saturday
10 May 1913 and could seat 650 (with no balcony). It was taken over by
Gaumont in 1927 and became part of the J. Arthur Rank organisation in 1942.
The last show was on Saturday 10 October 1959.

A wider view of the 'Pav', as it was affectionately known, sandwiched
between Henry Field's (milliners, tobacconists and hairdressers) and the New
White Horse Hotel. Far right is the Gold Street chambers of Cattell, Favell and
Hodge, a well-known firm of accountants, auditors, and insurance agents.

Two more recent photographs of the Lloyds Bank corner, one from the 1920s and the other probably from the late 1940s or early 50s. Well-known shops seen here include Freeman, Hardy & Willis, International Stores and Charnleys the opticians. Charnleys are still there, but Freeman, Hardy & Willis later moved to Gold Street.

There's a veritable hive of activity outside the Old White Horse Hotel (now
Burtons the tailors) in this photograph from 1914.

Gold Street

Gold Street, 1918, showing the commanding facade of the popular jeweller,
clothier and pawnbroker A.R. Brake. Mr Brake, a native of Marston Trussell,
came to Kettering in 1887 and began selling furniture, prams and pianos in a
range of 16 showrooms ~ a large trade done on a cash basis.

This view, from the early 1900s, looks back down Gold Street from Newland Street. On the right is the Fuller Chapel, named after the Revd Andrew Fuller (1754-1815), one of the driving forces behind the Baptist Movement and founder member of the Missionary Society in 1792. The church was built in 1860 at a cost of £4,000 by local firm Henson and Buswell.

An architect's drawing for the old Post Office buildings. The terracotta Gotch
and Saunders development opened in September 1887 and consisted of the
Post Office and seven shops. It was demolished in 1975 to make way for the
Newborough Centre, despite protests from the Civic Society
and a public enquiry.

An 1859 lithograph of the old Kettering Grammar School and master's residence, erected in 1856 and used as a school until 1913 when its 50 pupils moved to larger premises in Bowling Green Road (now the Council offices). It later became the house and surgery of Dr Daniel Drake-Lee, and for its final 20 years was the Council Surveyor's department, before being pulled down and replaced by shops in 1964.

The old Post Office Arcade during the 1930s. The archway (right) led through
to Richard Leys, Tanners Lane and Northall Street. The imposing building
was a dominant feature of Gold Street for three generations.

A rainy day in Gold Street in 1922. The old Grammar School can be seen in the distance, next to Elworthy's Crown Brewery, which closed a few years after this was picture was taken.

This magnificent picture, taken just before World War I, shows Gold Street
long before pedestrianised areas had to be created.

These two pictures show the freedom cyclists had back in 1908 and the 1920s. On the left, next to the Crown Inn, was the Victoria Picture Palace, which first became a picture house in 1920 and was wired for sound in 1929.

A rare picture of the old Victoria Hall before films were shown, published by Day's Stationery Store next door. The 'Vic' was officially opened on 17 December 1888, when the town's Choral Society performed *The Messiah*. It cost £6,000, could seat 1,000 people in stalls, balcony and gallery, and seats could be removed for dances and exhibitions. It became a full-time professional theatre in 1907, when musicals, plays and other professional entertainment were booked by Alf Bailey, who had a music shop in Gold Street.

The Victoria Picture Palace was replaced by the Odeon cinema in September 1936. The film *My Lucky Star*, with Richard Greene and Cesar Romero, was showing when this picture was taken two years later. The last show was Saturday 29 October 1960. It re-opened as a bingo hall, and in September 1974 it was demolished.

A man in uniform strides towards the camera in this well-populated view of post First World War Gold Street.

Shoppers pause to pose for the camera outside Hitchman's chemists on the corner
with Silver Street in 1909. This old-established family business began in the 1830s and
first made its base at three-storey premises in Market Place. Hitchman's made their
own sulphur pastilles, a special preparation for skin complaints such as eczema,
psoriasis and impetigo, as well as ulcers and acne. They were also well known for their
extract of honey "for soft and white hands" ~ sent to all parts of the UK and abroad.

A cold and lonely policeman keeps his feet warm with straw while on traffic duty at the Gold Street junction with Newland Street in this evocative picture from the 1920s.

Another bobby stands on traffic duty at the same junction before traffic lights were introduced. This was taken in front of the new three-storey Burtons store during the 1930s.

The final photograph in this Gold Street series shows a delivery boy and a lady with her pram standing outside Brakes.

Market Place

A near-deserted Market Place in the early 1900s, with the Market Hill buildings to the right in front of the church (now a car park). The Albion Temperance Hotel was demolished in 1936 and Payne's bakers and adjoining buildings, including the YMCA, followed two years later.

Two busy market days in Kettering, circa 1905. Kettering was first granted a weekly market to be held every Friday by Henry III in 1227.

An overhead view of Kettering market as goods are unpacked for display.

A policeman (centre) keeps a friendly eye on proceedings as shoppers flock
for bargains in 1904.

"Smile, please!" Townsfolk pose for the camera on the Market Place in 1906.
On the left is the stationery store owned by local photographer Herbert Evans,
who took many of the pictures in this book.

Three cheeky children get in on the act in this 1920 view of the market,
looking back towards the High Street.

An early two-seater Morris Minor (front right) is just one of ten splendid old motor cars captured in 1935. Behind are the premises of the Carrington Shoe Company and the Corn Exchange Billiard Saloon.

A delivery lorry unloads in this unusual 1926 view of the Market Place taken
from outside M. Coles, the tobacconists, next door to the Royal Hotel.

Old buildings next to the Albion Hotel in front of the Parish Church. The
house on the left, demolished in 1921, was occupied by William and Edward
Davidson, the watchmakers and gun dealers.

This photograph from the 50s was taken from the Royal Hotel looking
towards Sheep Street.

An empty Market Place around 1913. In the centre is Payne's the bakers and confectioners, established in the town in 1886 by Peterborough baker John Faulkner Payne. The Market Hill bakehouse was built in 1900 with two new ovens and other machinery driven by electric motor to produce pastries, fancy bread, biscuits, wedding cakes and pork pies. Note also English & American Teeth!

A super bird's eye view of the Market Place taken around 1912 from the tower
of the Parish Church. In the background you can see smoking chimneys in
front of the old gasworks.

Newland Street/Silver Street

Warren East's fine photograph of the Gold Street/Newland Street corner at the turn of the century. Well-known drapers Finlay & Co. proudly display their wares, including Union Jacks in the doorway!

A postcard view of Newland Street published around 1912 by H. Winstone,
stationer and tobacconist in the street. Finlays have been replaced by the
Northampton Rubber Company, which sold everything from mackintoshes,
waterproofs, rubber cycle tyres and hot water bottles to nursing aprons,
galoshes, trusses and elastic hosiery.

A look back along Newland Street from the direction of Rockingham Road in 1935. Jessops and Cobleys are among the shops on the right.

Newland Street in 1908. Buildings on the right include the Fleur de Lys public
house offering "Fine Ales and Stouts" and "Good Stabling".

This picture shows how narrow Silver Street was in the early part of the
century, with barely enough room for horses and carts
and early motor vehicles to pass.

A young man stands precariously on a ladder outside Frank Page's barber shop in 1909. Of the businesses on the right, only the Rising Sun public house and Chalkleys survive today.

This 1921 photograph shows a horse passing the Mikado Café in Newland
Street and Harry Taylor's cycle shop on the corner of Montagu Street and
Silver Street. Mr Taylor always kept a large stock of new machines, with
costlier models made to order.

Bicycles were a most popular mode of transport when this photograph of
Silver Street was taken in 1917. Mobbs the butchers is the shop on the right.

A young mother tries to negotiate the pavement with her pram in this second
view of Silver Street from 1917.

The imposing edifice of the former Wesleyan Chapel in Silver Street seen
through the lens of local photographer Herbert Evans. It cost £3,400 when it
was built in 1866 and could seat more than 600. The Council demolished it
when the road was widened in 1933 and built the Methodist Church in nearby
School Lane as a replacement.

A steamroller at work shortly before the 1933 demolition of the Wesleyan
Chapel. In a letter to the *Evening Telegraph*, local ministers
Revd Walter J. Ashton and Revd Gilbert S. Watts described the removal of
front coping stones and windows as "little short of sacrilege". Excited
workmen found a bottle, nestling in the foundation stone, which originally
contained church records. But the records had since rotted away, leaving just
two copper coins and some ashes!

Dalkeith Place and Horsemarket

There were no parking problems in this fine Edwardian view of Dalkeith
Place, Kettering, taken in 1908.

Dalkeith Place as it was around 1915. Dalkeith Billiards Hall, boasting
15 tables, and Dalkeith Arcade occupied the site formerly owned by
W.H. Staynes and Smith, leather merchants and importers. It later became
Watts the furnishers, and still stands.

Bosworth's cycle and motor bike shop and Henry Palmer's music stores are among the shops on the left of this 1914 view, looking to Silver Street from Dalkeith Place.

Dalkeith Place and Silver Street in 1880. Palmer's, established in 1875, were renowned for their range of musical instruments and sheet music. The family business also operated as an agent for His Master's Voice, selling early music recordings. It was in the town for almost 100 years.

The Cross Keys Café, erected in 1880, was named after the manorial sign of the Bishop of Peterborough. The restaurant could seat 180, split into first and second class dining rooms and ladies' dining rooms.

The Wesleyan Church formed an impressive backdrop to Dalkeith Place. Shops on the right included Bird & Tomkins the fruiterers and Cobleys the grocers.

The handsome Liberal Club, another Gotch and Saunders building, opened in
1889 to house the new Liberal Organisation. The Jacobean-style building,
which cost £3,400, boasted offices, a comfortable club, billiard room and
assembly hall for 200 persons. Public meetings were often addressed from the
balcony. It later became a bank, and is now a restaurant.

A closer view of Cross Keys Café. It, too, had a ground floor billiard room
plus a ballroom with sprung floor for parties, dances and other functions.
The proprietor for many years was Mr R.N. Tarry of Bugbrooke
who, with his wife, took over in 1903.

The Horsemarket, pictured here in the 1930s, was once known as Hog Leys,
because in former times it was covered in grass on which pigs would feed.
Later a horse fair was established, from which it took its name.
On the left of the picture is the old Parish Church School, now a taxi rank.

London Road

A horse-drawn cart goes slowly past the Pytchley Autocar Company in this 1913 photograph of London Road.

All the latest models on display outside the Pytchley Autocar Company.

A 1916 view of London Road hill, travelling away from the town.
At that time there was a brickworks at the bottom left and houses were yet to
be built on the right.

The symmetry of telegraph poles lends an artistic aspect to this 1915 photograph. It was taken facing the town ~ the opposite direction to the picture on page 94.

Cattle being herded to market in 1905 past the London Road Congregational
Church watched by a group of children at the top of St Peter's Avenue.

A view of the old Kettering police station in 1944. This sprawling but
attractive building, erected in 1851, has long since been replaced by a more
modern complex incorporating the new magistrates courts.

The old workhouse building in London Road (now St Mary's Hospital) was
built in 1837 for £6,000 and could accommodate 300 inmates. A new infirmary
and laundry were added in 1894 and the top two storeys of the centre block
were demolished in May 1971.

A 1907 view of London Road. The girl pushing the pram is passing in front of
the police station.

The former Cattle Market in London Road after it was enlarged in 1906, with
the parish church in the background. The site, now a car park, was opened in
1880 at a cost of £8,000, and markets selling fatstock were held there every
Friday until it moved to Northfield Avenue in 1967. It closed after more than a
century of operation in March 1992.

Taken on 28 March 1916 this picture of London Road shows the results
(including snapped telegraph poles!) of an unusually severe blizzard that had
hit the town. It was the worst snowstorm for more than 40 years, trees were
uprooted and buses and trains brought to a standstill.

Rockingham Road

What horse-drawn traffic there was just after the turn of the century didn't
seem to worry these children playing or just standing in Rockingham Road.

The proud tower of Rockingham Road School (right) and the nearby
Electricity Works chimney dominate this street scene in Rockingham Road,
looking towards the town centre circa 1910.

A street entertainer plays his barrel organ in Rockingham Road in 1915.
The sandwich board on the left is advertising Charles Usher, the
High Street jeweller.

Two of Kettering's long-gone public houses ~ the Hare and Hounds and The
Vine (next door) ~ stood on part of the site now occupied by
Sainsbury's superstore.

The Rockingham Road junction with King Street (right) has changed very little since the turn of the century.

Learner & Woodward, Barlow's, Harrison's and Letts & Son are among the shops on the right in this wider view of Rockingham Road.

This sunny scene from 1923 shows the former Wesleyan Church on the corner
of Regent Street. The chapel, later to become the headquarters of the local
Salvation Army, could seat up to 600 worshippers.

Wicksteed Park

The Lake

Wicksteed Park

Wicksteed Park, Kettering

Wicksteed Park, Kettering

The Lake

The Lodge

An early postcard of Wicksteed Park taken just a few years after it officially
opened to the public in 1921 on meadowland between
Kettering and Barton Seagrave.

News of the country's first leisure park soon spread far and wide, and
charabancs and special trains brought excited crowds from out of town.
By 1930 there were a million summer visitors.

Early day-trippers to Wicksteed Park could enjoy teas on the lawn served by
this wood-built canteen, pictured in 1928.

A total of 600 diners could be accommodated when the pavilion was extended. This building has been improved many times over the years and has become a popular venue for company dinner and dances, now seating up to 1,700.

This view of the pavilion shows the clock given to the park by the Clubmen of
Kettering. In 1928 park founder Charles Wicksteed designed a unique
machine which could both slice and butter bread at the rate of 2,000 slices an
hour to feed hungry visitors.

The sunken gardens at "Wickies".

The statue in the gardens erected in memory of
Mr Wicksteed's beloved pet dog Jerry

Part of the children's playground and sandpit pictured in the 1920s. The swings and slides were designed by Charles Wicksteed and later exported to more than 70 countries.

The "giant chute", pictured here in 1930, was among the many unusual pieces
of play equipment which children could enjoy free of charge.
The famous "waterchute" was introduced in the early 1920s
and soon became the star attraction.

Visitors enjoy boating on Wicksteed Park's 30-acre lake. It was opened in 1921
with a handful of rowing boats. The present day fleet numbers more than 100.

The miniature railway still runs regularly around the lake. The two original
engines are called King Arthur and the Lady of the Lake.

Endless hours of fun could be had on the swings and roundabouts, which
were novelties to many youngsters. This part of the park, now boasting more
modern activity equipment, remains free to children.

A couple, complete with pram and family dog, enjoy a stroll past the gardens
in the 1930s.

More Street Scenes

Headlands has always been one of Kettering's more impressive tree-lined thoroughfares with large houses on either side.

Skid marks on the road show the dangers of venturing out in this wintry
scene of Headlands in April 1908.

Traffic lights now control this busy Stamford Road junction, part of the town's
one-way system. Bindley's fruit store (left) on the corner of Eskdaill Street is
now Glover's cycle shop. The old Stamford Road School (centre) is the
William Knibb Centre, while Munn's is now a lawn in front of
the Jehovah's Witnesses Hall.

This 1921 photograph was taken further along Stamford Road looking down
the hill towards the Bath Road junction. A sign on the right advertises a riding
school for would-be cyclists!

Montagu Street in the 1930s, including the Co-op's central store and arcade.
For more than 40 years the Central Hall, seating 600 downstairs and 250 in the
balcony, was used for dances, stage shows and business functions. The
legendary Joe Davis won the World Snooker Final when it was
staged there in 1934.

A closer look at the KICS complex in the late 1920s. It included the Lutona
sweet shop and a ladies' and gentlemen's hairdressers
next to Robinson's garage.

United Counties buses pick up passengers outside the library in Sheep Street
during the late 1920s. The company was formed from the Wellingborough
Motor Omnibus Company, which was incorporated in 1913.

A bustling Sheep Street outside the George Hotel in 1919. The George was
built on the site of a pub called the Cock, dating back to the 1600s. Its facilities
included stables, two coach houses, a cow house and a pig yard!

The old British School, pictured in 1908 but dating from 1874. The building in School Lane is now the Four Seasons Day Centre.

The former Wesleyan Church on the corner of Rockingham Road and Regent Street, pictured here in 1905.

The London Road Congregational Church on the corner of St Peter's Avenue
in 1915. Built in 1898, it was formed after a split between
the Revd J.M. Watson and more influential members of Toller Chapel.
The photograph shows a wonderfully ornate street lamp.

Two views looking up Station Road towards the town centre, both around 1910. The second one (right) shows the Waverley Hotel on the left. Horse-drawn transport also provided a regular service from the railway station to the George and Royal.

A look down one of Kettering's prouder, but by no means proudest,
residential streets ~ Broadway in 1905.

A horse-drawn Barlow's bread van stops to make door-to-door deliveries in
St Peter's Avenue. The firm of Henry Barlow and Son was a well-established
local baker which had Kettering branches until the 1980s. This picture was
taken in 1926.

The grand Primitive Methodist Church in Bath Road, erected in 1906 at a cost of £5,000. The building, which had pews for 700, now has a new frontage and is part of the Timson Perfecta engineering works.

Local worshippers are seen leaving the Primitive Methodist Church, with the Revds Clifford, Wellburn and Bicheno on the steps.

Kettering General Hospital can just be seen behind trees in Rothwell Road in 1913. The hospital was built in 1896 at a cost of £18,101 and opened the following year. The five-acre site was donated by the Duke of Buccleuch, and a ward still bears his name.

This rural scene at the bottom of Rothwell Road in 1905 is the site now
occupied by the Northfield Avenue roundabout. The field on the left is now
Do-It-All's DIY store, and in the distance you can see the chimney from
Thomas Geary's leather works.

Timpson's boot and shoe factory in Bath Road, built in splendid isolation in 1922. It operated as a family concern for 50 years before being taken over by the British Shoe Corporation.

Kettering Iron and Coal Company's blast furnaces, a mile north of the railway station, were demolished in 1963 after having closed in 1959. Quarrying began off Rockingham Road in 1878, initially with two furnaces each producing 250 tons of iron a week. A third was built 20 years later but was replaced by a much larger furnace in 1908, when a second chimney was erected.

A flagpole is erected using an extending ladder in this unusual old photograph of Carrington Street, showing the Angel Hotel on the left.

People and Events

The official opening of Kettering Public Library in Sheep Street on
7 May 1904. It was built for £8,500 thanks to the well-known benefactor
Andrew Carnegie, who attended the ceremony.

Kettering people adored taking part in parades and festivities. This one,
heading along the High Street to the Market Place, was the Baptist Sunday
School treat of 1906, with Oakley Street proudly to the fore.

Fuller Church and the Primitive Methodist Church are among the Sunday
Schools represented at this Treat Day gathering on the Market Place in 1907.
Three ladies are seen looking out from the balcony of the stationers shop run
by Herbert Evans, who took this group picture.

India was the theme for this float in the High Street procession to celebrate the Coronation of George V in 1911. The horse-drawn tableau with its splendid model of the Taj Mahal is attended by men and women in Indian costume.

Moving in the opposite direction is this lively carnival parade from the early 1900s. The ladies in white are from the Temperance Movement, which was very strong in Kettering at that time. Their hall in Gold Street opened in 1864 and could seat 250 people.

In 1906 it was Kettering's turn to host the annual agricultural show. To mark the occasion two spectacular archways were erected, one outside the George Hotel (right) and the other at the top of Montagu Street (above). They were erected by Walter "King" Toseland, florist and seedsman, of Newland Street.

A daylight picture of the Sheep Street archway outside a flag-festooned
George Hotel. The heads of cattle in each corner of the archway were painted
by Tommy Moisey, commercial artist, of Queen Street. The shop on the left
was kept by Joseph Emerson, pastrycook and confectioner, who moved there
from High Street when the road was widened (see page 10).

Many public gatherings and political meetings were held on the Market Place and addressed from the Palace Cinema (formerly the Corn Exchange), erected in 1853. The cavalry join the throng for this intriguing event at which the Union Jack is displayed alongside the Japanese flag, probably towards the end of World War I.

A horse-drawn steam fire engine leads a parade of firemen leaving the Market
Place on 7 July 1911. Behind them is the premises of Berry Bros. & Bagshaw,
the auctioneers and estate agents, built two years earlier.

Six shire horses pulled a lifeboat around town during Lifeboat Day in 1908.
They are seen here in Sheep Street, passing between the Dryland Memorial
and the George Hotel's stable block.

People gather on the Market Place to witness the start of the lifeboat
procession, which finished at the Furnace Reservoir in Rockingham Road,
where children were given penny rides by crewmen.

Wallis and Linnell wagonettes gather for the clothing company's Jubilee Outing on 7 July 1906. The firm once owned six factories in the area and boasted that it was the first in town to use the typewriter, install internal phones and adopt a Tannoy system.

Roll up for all the fun of the fair! This picture of Kettering Feast in 1902 shows
the two bioscope shows, the one on the left was owned by William Taylor and
the other by Charles Thurston. The cost to see these early picture shows was
two old pence.

Kettering's carnival was always a colourful and well-attended festivity. These fancy dress participants, pictured in London Road around 1910, brought their bicycles along for the ride.

The local fire service and a brass band were among those taking part in this
parade along Regent Street. The shop on the corner of Wellington Street was
P. Thomas the grocers.

Special Constables, assigned to despatch rider duties, astride their
motorcycles at the rear of the police station in the 1920s. Although in 'civvies',
each sports an official armband and all but two have temporary 'POLICE'
stickers on their headlamps. It is possible that this was during the
General Strike in 1926.

Musical pierrots were a popular attraction at Wicksteed Park's bandstand
during the 1920's. One such group was Bits O' Brightness, with piano
supplied by Palmer's music store.

A brass band heads a Temperance procession approaching the top of Gold Street in 1906. To the right of Fuller Church is the home and surgery of Dr John Allison who was the Council's Medical Officer of Health from 1906 until his retirement in 1930.

A somewhat faded photograph captures the same procession as it marches along High Street towards Bakehouse Hill.

Military parades always attract a crowd of enthusiastic onlookers, as these two pictures show.

Townsfolk turn out in the Market Place to witness a parade of volunteers destined eventually to see active service during World War I. Some 720 men were to lose their lives, their names later being engraved on the War Memorial tablets outside the Art Gallery.

A rare picture of the first World War I memorial service outside Kettering
Library on 11 November 1919. The temporary wooden cenotaph was used
until the stone one was unveiled beside the Art Gallery in 1921.

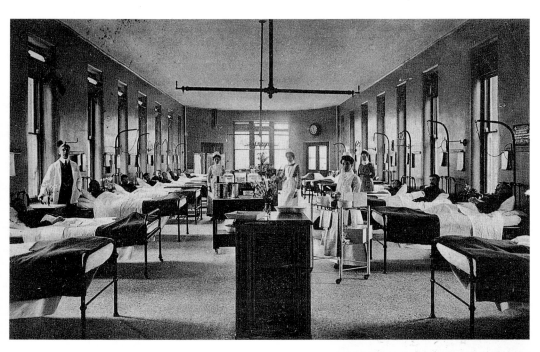

The men's ward and children's ward at Kettering General Hospital in 1909. The hospital had 58 beds in its three wards plus an outpatients department for eye cases and surgical appliances.

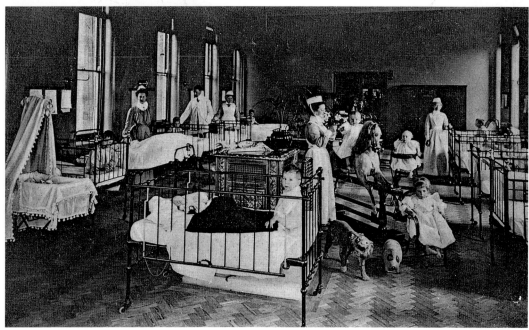

Police help control the crowds which flocked to the Victoria Hall in Gold
Street for a three-day sale organised by the local Red Cross in 1915.
The proceeds went to World War I refugees from Belgium who were billeted
in the town.

It was a full house at the Geisha tea rooms at the proclamation of King George V
on the Market Place on 11 May 1910. Vint's Electric Palace had opened the
previous October and was renamed the Palace when John Covington took it
over in 1912.

Thousands of local children put on their Sunday best to assemble in the
Manor House Field for the Coronation festivities in 1911, their Union Jacks
and St George's flags on display.

LONG LIVE THE KING

Headlands Arch, Kettering. Coronation. 1911.

A picture of King George V overlooks this wonderful archway erected in
Headlands for the Coronation.

One of the highlights of the Coronation festivities locally was the huge street party and children's tea in Headlands, with boaters and bonnets the order of the day for parents.

Keeping clothes and linen clean was a problem in the days before washing machines, when coal was used in open fires and soot got everywhere. Kettering Steam Laundry in Church Walk promised to dry-clean any article from a necktie to a suite of furniture!

The London Central Meat Company was a well-known butcher's shop on the corner of High Street and Huxloe Place. As can be seen in this picture, taken in 1904, steak was priced at 7d per lb, and chops at 6d.

Kettering District

This splendid bus stops outside the Green Dragon in Broughton en route to Northampton in 1914. This picture was taken by village photographer Horace Baxter. The Green Dragon later became a bakery and is now a private house.

This photograph shows two young ladies looking over the Ise brook at the old Barton bridge in 1907. In the distance is Barton Seagrave Church.

Children gather at the junction of Church Street and Meeting Lane in Burton Latimer in 1906. The building on the left is a doctor's surgery, and on the right, next to the Thatcher's Arms in Church Street, is the blacksmith's house.

Customers sit outside the Red Lion in Cranford in the early 1900s. The pub is believed to date back to 1680.

Northamptonshire folk loved to join in country pursuits such as shooting and hunting. This photograph by Herbert Evans shows the Pytchley Hounds at Pytchley before World War I.

Sir Thomas Tresham's market house in Rothwell was begun in 1577, but Sir Thomas died before the roof was on, and roofless it remained for more than 300 years, when it was finished by John Alfred Gotch.

Rothwell's famous bone crypt, beneath the Parish Church, contains 4,000 bones and skulls, collected down the centuries from an overcrowded churchyard. Some go back to the 13th century, before wooden coffins were used for burials.

Huge crowds gather in 1928 for the traditional proclamation to open Rowell Fair, which is still held today. In their midst, protected by spear-holding halbardiers, is the representative of the Lord of the Manor who, at certain points, stops his horse to read the ancient charter.

High Street, Desborough in 1920, looking towards the church and showing Sketchley Cleaners opposite a newsagent selling *The Kettering Leader*.

Children casually wander along Station Road, Desborough in the early part of the century.

Count the hats! This marvellous photograph shows the celebrations to mark
the signing of peace, in Desborough on 19 July 1919.

Coronation festivities in Geddington in 1911.
Members of Geddington Band march along Bridge
Street towards the cross.

Desborough youngsters (and their dogs) mill
around the old village "cross", a square pillar
used as a signpost with place names and
distances to London, Kettering and
Harborough painted on its sides. Opposite is
the George Hotel and (far right)
the King's Arms.

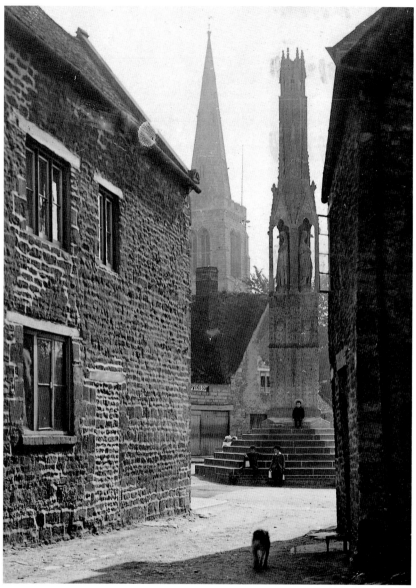

The 40-ft high Queen Eleanor Cross at Geddington, pictured (left) in 1907 and, from an unusual angle, next to the Star Inn in 1932. It was one of 12 crosses erected by Edward I to mark the resting places of Queen Eleanor's body on her last journey to Westminster in 1290.

Ducks paddle on the brook running through picturesque Grafton Underwood
in 1911. The village was to become well known as the air base for the first
American bombers in Britain during World War II.